The Swiss Re Cookbook
for the NSPCC

Edited by Tee Dobinson

6/12/13

For Ratna

Regards

Tee Dobinson

X

Neshath Rahman

Age 11

Contents

Melissa Steeger
Age 8

Valentin Lita
Age 7

Introduction from Russell Higginbotham

As part of our support for the NSPCC as our Charity of the Year' in 2011 and 2012, we decided to produce a cookbook featuring recipes from the Swiss Re team in the UK. I was delighted to receive recipes from some of our most senior Group executives, and also a fabulous range of contributions from my local colleagues. The range of dishes in this cookbook really illustrates the diverse culture of the Swiss Re team.

We were also very pleased to get contributions from Esther Rantzen, CBE, the Founder and President of ChildLine and good friend of Swiss Re, and the broadcaster and journalist Fiona Bruce. It was fantastic that Arnaud Stevens, Executive Head Chef from the Searcys restaurant at the top of 'The Gherkin', took time out from his kitchen to give us an insight into preparing a professional dish.

As a full £10 from each book sold goes to the NSPCC, we felt that it was particularly apt to have it illustrated by children. We have some beautiful drawings created by children from Swiss Re families and we are proud to have collaborated with William Davis Primary School, who contributed all of the drawings of our iconic office building, adding something very special to our book.

Thank you for purchasing this cookbook. Your contribution supports the amazing work of the NSPCC. I also sincerely hope that you enjoy the fabulous dishes, many of which are long-held family favourite recipes.

With best wishes

Russell Higginbotham
CEO Swiss Re UK & Ireland

Lucy Higginbotham
Age 4
Drawing of Russell

Rufaidah Husain
Age 7½

Swiss Re UK and the NSPCC

In 2010 Swiss Re employees in the UK voted the NSPCC as their 'Charity of the Year' for a two-year partnership in 2011 and 2012. The specific goal of the Swiss Re employees' initiative is to raise funds for the NSPCC's two national helplines that offer round-the-clock support, and help to protect children from abuse and neglect.

In 2011, **£241,376** was raised by Swiss Re employees. Half of the funds raised are being used to recruit and train 75 volunteer ChildLine counsellors who, between them, can respond to over 15,600 children in need in just one year. The remaining funds have contributed to the development of the NSPCC's text service for adults concerned about a child. Thanks to the support of Swiss Re employees the public is now able to contact the NSPCC anonymously via text message, helping to protect even more children from abuse and neglect. At its launch, 40% of users said they would not have contacted the NSPCC without the text service.

Mike Parker, Director of Fundraising NSPCC comments:
"This support from Swiss Re is so important to the NSPCC, allowing us to help prevent child cruelty. The partnership is proving a fantastic success. Swiss Re employees have really got behind activities and contributed to some great initiatives such as this cookbook. We hope to raise almost £20,000 from this first edition of 'The Swiss Re Cookbook for the NSPCC' and this funding will enable us to give vulnerable children the support they so desperately need."

Anyone with concerns about a child should call the **NSPCC** on 0808 800 5000. They can also email help@nspcc.org.uk or make a report online at www.nspcc.org.uk/helpline **and now text on 88858**

Children and young people can contact **ChildLine** any time to talk. Calls are free and confidential on 0800 1111 or visit our website www.childline.org.uk

Sumaiyah Choudhury
Age 10

Why is This Cookbook Illustrated by Gherkins?

Plans for this cookbook began with a competition to find the best recipes. Some employees added an illustration to their recipes and we also asked pupils from William Davis Primary School, situated close to the Swiss Re offices in The Gherkin, to help us by providing additional illustrations.

At the school, editor Tee Dobinson asked some children to start by drawing The Gherkin. They responded so enthusiastically that Tee decided that every child in the school, aged three to eleven, would draw the building.

We all liked the idea of using the children's illustrations of The Gherkin in our cookbook and you will see 82 of them spread throughout the book.

We hope you enjoy their multi-coloured and imaginative interpretations.

Tahia Ahmed
Age 4

Mahin Ahmed
Age 10

Mains

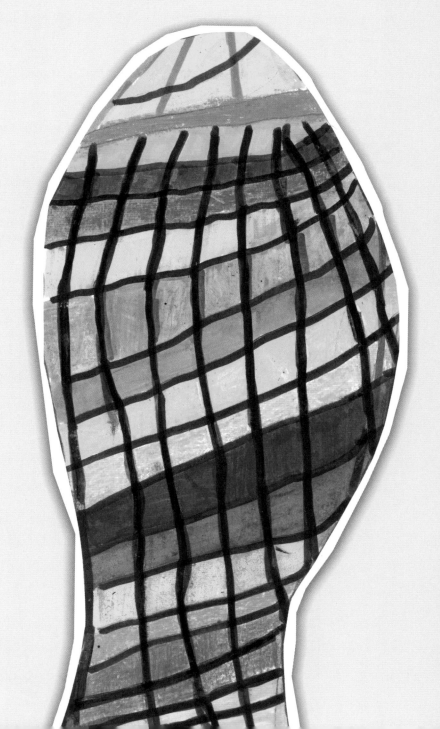

Sumaiya Yasmin
Age 9

Esther's Fish Pie

"This is ideal comfort food! We love it for family suppers."

Esther Rantzen, CBE, Founder and President of ChildLine

Ingredients
(Serves 4)
→ 2 lb potatoes boiled and mashed with butter and milk, salt and pepper (or ready-made mash!)
→ 2 lb haddock or cod (smoked fish will give a much stronger flavour)
→ 1 pint milk
→ 4 oz butter
→ 2 oz flour
→ 4 hard boiled eggs, chopped
→ 4 tablespoons fresh chopped parsley
→ 2 tablespoons fresh lemon juice
→ Salt and black pepper

Method
Preheat the oven to 200°C.

Place fish in a shallow baking dish, pour over half the milk and bake for 15 minutes at 200°C. Flake into large pieces.

Make a white sauce: melt butter in pan, add flour gradually, stirring constantly and cook over low heat for 4–5 minutes. Do not let the mixture boil.

Stir remaining milk including fish liquid into the white sauce and add salt and pepper. Mix to a smooth consistency and cook for a further two minutes.

Add flaked fish to sauce, together with eggs, parsley, lemon and season to taste.

Put fish mixture into baking dish large enough to hold 2 ½ pints. Spread the mashed potatoes over the top and fork a pattern on the fish pie.

Bake in oven at 200 °C for about 30 minutes until golden brown. Top with sprigs of parsley.

Serve with fresh vegetables.

Note: For ounces to grams conversion see chart on page 90

Amelie Higginbotham
Age 6
Drawing of Esther

Ajmal Miah
Age 3

Roast Salmon with Garlic and Rosemary and Zingy Bacon Potatoes

"This is one of my favourite dinners to make after work (to make it even easier switch the potatoes for brown rice, then it's super healthy as well as delicious). A bottle of Riesling or Sauvignon Blanc goes down very well with it ... enjoy and cheers!"

Alison Martin, *Head of Life & Health Reinsurance, Group Management Board*

Ingredients
(Serves 2)
→ 2 salmon fillets
→ Garlic clove thinly sliced
→ Sprig of rosemary
→ Olive oil
→ Sea salt and black pepper
→ Small bag of new potatoes (enough for two, or make extra and have the next day, still yummy)
→ 2–3 rashers streaky bacon (omit if you're not into meat)
→ 10–20 cherry tomatoes
→ 1 red onion finely chopped
→ 1 tablespoon olive oil
→ 1 teaspoon white wine vinegar
→ 1 teaspoon grainy mustard (if you really like mustard then add a bit more)
→ Oregano or other herbs of your choice
→ Broccoli or other green vegetable (it's good to have lots of colour!)

Method
Preheat the oven to 180°C.

Wash new potatoes and halve/quarter so you have smallish and equal pieces. Boil in hot water with a pinch of salt for 15–20 minutes until they are soft (test with a knife – if it goes through easily they are done). Drain and leave in pan with lid on to keep warm.

Whilst potatoes are boiling, chop tomatoes in halves and spread onto baking tray, seeds up, drizzle with olive oil, generous helping of sea salt and black pepper and whatever herb you fancy – oregano works well but am sure others do. Whack in the oven for about 15 minutes until they have started to ooze a bit, you might want to keep in for another 5 minutes depending on how soft you like your tomatoes.

Meanwhile, grill streaky bacon until well done (or fry), then chop into small pieces, drain off excess fat on a paper towel and leave to one side.

Fry chopped onion in olive oil until just starting to soften, turn off heat, add white wine vinegar and mustard then tip in potatoes and mix well. Don't add the bacon yet ...

To prep the salmon, lay out a largish piece of tinfoil and put the salmon fillets on such that you will be able to fold as a parcel. Add sliced garlic, rosemary (if you can gently push the garlic and rosemary into the fish the flavours will infuse better), a dash of olive oil, sprinkle of sea salt and black pepper. Fold up in a parcel and then put on a baking tray in the oven for 12–15 minutes.

Boil broccoli for 5–6 minutes towards the end of the salmon cooking time so that it's ready when the fish comes out of the oven.

As you're serving everything add the bacon to the potatoes and mix well.

*The potatoes are influenced by the domestic goddess, Nigella Lawson, herself ...

Siddika Nazifa
Age 5

Shakil Mahtey
Age 8

Cornwall Crab Cakes and Pumpkin Soup

"This is a beautiful recipe for spring and summer and could be a wonderful dish for your dinner party."

Arnaud Stevens, *Executive Head Chef Searcys | The Gherkin & Group Development Chef*

Ingredients
(Serves 6)
Crab Cakes
→ 400 g dry mashed potatoes
→ 400 g flour
→ 400 g breadcrumbs
→ 250 g fresh picked white crab meat
→ 135 g cooked salmon
→ 100 g butter
→ 10 eggs, beaten
→ 1 onion, chopped
→ ½ head of fennel, diced
→ 6 teaspoons fresh coriander
→ 6 teaspoons chopped parsley
→ 2 teaspoons whole grain mustard

Pumpkin Soup
→ 500 g vegetable broth
→ 200 g pumpkin
(or butternut squash)
→ 100 g butter
→ 100 g cream
→ 50 g onions
→ 3 teaspoons caster sugar
→ 1 teaspoon fresh red chilli, chopped
→ 1 teaspoon garlic, chopped
→ 1 teaspoon ginger, grated
→ Pinch of saffron
→ Dash of lime juice

Method
Pumpkin Soup
First dice the pumpkin then sweat with the onion, ginger and garlic in butter.

Add pumpkin mix to the vegetable broth. Bring to the boil and simmer until cooked. Add the sugar, saffron, fresh red chilli and a dash of lime juice. Blend the cream into the soup.

Crab Cakes
Put the peeled potatoes in a large pot and cover with water. Add salt and simmer until tender and just cooked. Drain in a colander, and allow the potatoes to dry slightly. Pass them through a potato ricer and set to one side. Weigh out the potatoes to ensure you have 400 g.

Cook the fennel and the onion in butter in a large non-stick pot until they are cooked down and translucent, season with salt and pepper to taste, add the herbs and allow to cool. In a clean mixing bowl blend together the cooked salmon, onions, fennel and herbs, then add the crab. Then stir in the potatoes and the mustard. Check the seasoning, and add salt and pepper if needed.

Using a set of scales weigh out 60 g portions. Form each one into a ball, coat with flour, dip briefly in the beaten eggs then coat with breadcrumbs to create the thin crispy outer layer. Heat some vegetable oil to 170°C, and fry the crab cakes for 4–5 minutes or until golden brown.

To serve, place a few crab cakes in each soup bowl, and pour the pumpkin soup around them.

Ben Morris
Age 12
Drawing of Arnaud

Perch Fillets in Saffron Sauce

"The only fish recipe I have actually managed to cook several times successfully … and I was positively surprised each time. So if you have no clue about cooking, have little time and still want to impress, try this one!"

Christian Mumenthaler, *CEO Reinsurance*

Ingredients
→ *200 g perch fillets (or can use seabass)*
→ *500 ml vegetable stock*
→ *500 g leeks*
→ *1 shallot, finely chopped*
→ *200 ml dry white wine*
→ *Freshly ground pepper*
→ *pinch of salt*
→ *2 tablespoons dry vermouth*
→ *150 ml double cream*
→ *salt and pepper to taste*
→ *saffron threads*

Method
Remove any remaining bones in the perch fillets and then slice them in half along the length of the fish.

Chop the leeks into small sections and cook in the vegetable stock for five minutes.

Drain leeks, reserving the cooking liquid. Keep leeks covered.

Add the white wine, the chopped shallot and a pinch of salt to 100 ml of the cooking liquid. Poach the perch in this for 5–7 minutes at just under boiling point.

Take the fillets out and keep covered. Again, keep the cooking liquid!

To make the sauce, strain the cooking liquid and add the vermouth. Simmer slowly until reduced to 4 tablespoonfuls.

Stir in the cream and saffron, heat very gently – do not boil. Season to taste.

Serve the fillets on a bed of leeks, spoon over the sauce and use a few leeks to garnish.

Oliver Price
Age 10
Drawing of Christian

Diana Lita
Age 4

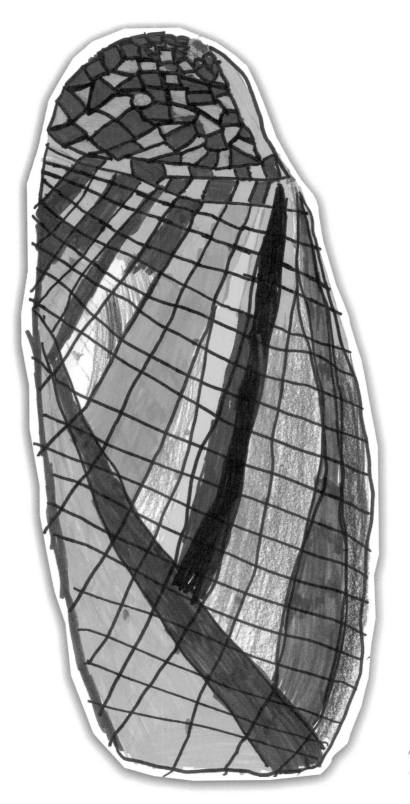

Mursheda Begum
Age 6

Baked Prawns with Feta and Tomatoes

"This is a fantastic, flavoursome, nice and simple dinner/snack. Thanks to my good friend Caroline, this has really helped assuage the hunger pains at the end of a long working day. Do use good quality tomatoes."

Lorraine Sage, Senior Communications Manager

Ingredients

(Serves 2)
→ 400g tiger or king prawns
→ 100ml dry white wine
→ 75g feta cheese
→ 1 medium onion, chopped
→ 1 tin chopped tomatoes
→ 3 tablespoons olive oil
→ 2 tablespoons fresh parsley
→ 1 teaspoon oregano
→ Salt and pepper to taste

Method

Preheat the oven to 180°C.

Sauté the chopped onion until translucent.

Add the wine and boil for 3−4 minutes (the majority of the wine will evaporate).

Add the tomatoes and oregano. Season with salt and pepper to taste.

Shell the prawns (or buy prawns that are already prepared).

Add the prawns and parsley to the sauce.

Put the mixture into a baking dish and sprinkle with cheese.

Bake for 20 minutes.

Serve with crusty bread and salad.

Amelia Thompson
Age 8
Drawing of Lorraine

Teriyaki Chicken

"This is my recipe for teriyaki chicken, I just cooked it tonight – put rice on your plate, the chicken on the rice, dribble the sauce over the chicken – and there you are!"

Fiona Bruce, *TV Broadcaster and Journalist*

Ingredients
(Serves 2)
→ *2 chicken breasts cut into cubes*
→ *Basmati rice*

Sauce
→ *4 tablespoons soya sauce*
→ *4 tablespoons runny honey*
→ *4 tablespoons toasted sesame oil*
→ *2 teaspoons Tabasco sauce*
→ *A squeeze of lime*

Method
Mix all the sauce ingredients together and marinate the chicken in it (ideally for an hour or more – but a short time will suffice if necessary).

Start cooking the rice.

When the rice is nearly done, thread the chicken onto two skewers and grill for 10 minutes, turning once.

Boil the marinade in a saucepan until it is reduced, it should be thick and sticky.

Serve the chicken on rice with sauce dribbled over it.

Fiona Oakley
Age 11
Drawing of Fiona

Melissa Waskowska
Age 8

Mehbub Rahman
Age 9

Yvonne's Chicken Wrapped in Pastry

"I like to serve this with baby spinach and mango salad splashed with a touch of fine olive oil and thick balsamic vinegar. If you have any left over pastry you can use any cookie cutters you may have to create pastry decorations to pop on top of the parcels."

Yvonne Aeberhard Stutz, *Project Manager*

Ingredients

(Serves 2)
→ *2 boneless chicken breasts*
→ *2 heaped tablespoons flavoured cream cheese*
→ *4 slices Prosciutto ham*
→ *2 teaspoons grainy mustard*
→ *2 sheets of flaky pastry (or enough to wrap all around the chicken)*
→ *1 egg yolk, beaten with a little water*

Method

Preheat the oven to 200°C.

Take the chicken breasts and cut into one side of each – being careful not to cut right through. Stuff the opening generously with flavoured cream cheese – I like to use Boursin.

Wrap each breast with two slices of Prosciutto ham, tucking the ends under the chicken.

Take one sheet of flaky pastry and place each breast on it side by side, leaving some space around. Put a little of the grainy mustard under each breast, on the pastry.

Cut around the pastry leaving a margin around the chicken breasts. Brush the pastry around the chicken with the egg mixture and then place the second piece of pastry on top to make the parcel.

Press the pastry together using a fork. Brush the tops of the pastry packages with the remaining egg mixture.

Add pastry shape decorations to the top if you wish.

Place in the preheated oven at 200°C for 20–30 minutes until the pastry is golden.

To serve, cut each package in half and serve on plate at an angle.

Hainese Chicken Rice

"Hainese Chicken Rice is a dish that is very famous in a number of Far East Asian countries. It encompasses simple yet powerful ingredients to create a hearty and fulfilling dish. This dish can essentially be split into three separate parts – the chicken, the rice and the sauce. All of which are equally important!"

Hon Chan, *Upstream Energy Underwriter*

Ingredients

(Serves 2 hungry people)
→ *2 thighs/breasts per person (minimum 4 pieces otherwise the chicken stock will be weak)*
→ *150–250 g rice per person (American long grain)*
→ *6 stalks of spring onion*
→ *1 ½ heads of garlic*
→ *200–250 g ginger*
→ *Half a cucumber*
→ *1 lime*
→ *½ tablespoon sugar*
→ *3 tablespoons olive oil*
→ *salt to season*
→ *A little coriander (optional)*
→ *6 tablespoons of Sri Racha sauce (widely available in your local Asian store and some major supermarkets)*

Method

Chop the spring onion stalks into sizeable chunks. Next peel a large stalk of ginger and slice into similar size chunks to the spring onions. Before carrying on, put the desired amount of rice into water to soak – the reason will become apparent later.

Place the chicken pieces into a pot of seasoned water along with the ginger and spring onions. Bring to the boil and leave this to simmer slowly for 10–12 minutes while you prepare the garlic. Take a bulb and a half of garlic and chop finely, this will be used for the rice and sauce later.

Once the chicken has cooked, drain the meat and vegetables but make sure you keep your beautiful chicken stock! This is the basis of the whole meal!

Take a heavy duty non-stick pot and heat three tablespoons of olive oil. Next add 80% of the chopped garlic that was prepared earlier and fry gently and wait until it turns golden brown, then drain off the oil. Drain the water from the rice and add the soaked rice to the garlic and fry together. The reason for soaking the rice is so that it starts to absorb the water and therefore absorbs the garlic flavour much more intensely.

Continue frying for 2 minutes until most of the water from the rice has evaporated, then pour in the aromatic chicken stock from earlier into the rice, enough to cover the rice by about 2 cm. Bring to the boil and then turn down the heat, at this stage you can add in a little coriander if you like. Place the lid on and cook for 5–7 minutes.

Now the key phase of this meal – the sauce! Put a good six table-spoons of Sri Racha sauce into a bowl. Squeeze a quarter of a lime and add the remainder of the chopped garlic. Add half a tablespoon of sugar and season lightly with salt. Now add three tablespoons of the chicken stock, stir well and taste to test – there should be a noticeable kick with a tart and sweet aftertaste.

Slice your chicken and put on the plates, drizzle the sauce sparingly over the chicken and add rice as desired.

Serve with some cut cucumber for palate cleansing and a young Gavi di Gavi with high citrus notes to compliment the sauce, but light enough not to overpower the stunningly fragrant rice.

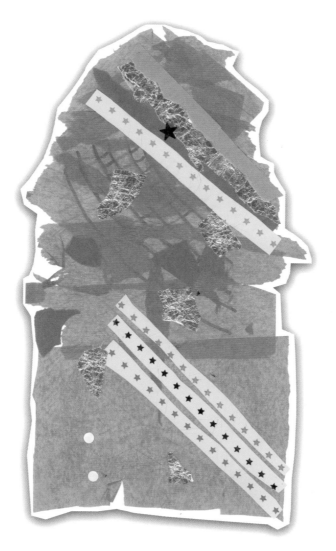

Nisfa Monowara
Age 10

Pesto and Mozzarella Chicken Wrapped in Parma Ham

"... on a warm summer evening, served with a fiery tomato salad, warmed ciabatta and a chilled glass of crisp white wine!"

Justin Excell, *Head of Rates, Group Management Board*

Ingredients
(Serves 2)
→ *2 chicken breasts*
→ *1 packet of Mozzarella*
→ *4 slices Parma ham*
→ *4 teaspoons fresh pesto*
→ *2 teaspoons olive oil*
→ *Freshly ground black pepper and salt*

Salad
→ *3 ripe beef tomatoes*
→ *1 large mild red chilli*
→ *2 handfuls of fresh rocket*
→ *1 tablespoon of fresh basil, roughly torn*
→ *1 tablespoon balsamic vinegar*
→ *1 tablespoon extra virgin olive oil*
→ *Juice of ½ lime*
→ *Freshly ground black pepper and salt*

Method
Preheat the oven to 200°C.

Butterfly the chicken breasts (partially slice through and open out flat). Spread the pesto across the opened surface of each chicken breast. Slice the Mozzarella and lay on top of the pesto, season and fold the chicken breast back together.

Wrap two slices of Parma ham around each chicken breast – use a cocktail stick to hold together if necessary (but remove before serving). Season with black pepper again.

In a medium-sized frying pan, heat the oil and sear the chicken breasts until golden.

Transfer to an oven dish and cook for 15 minutes in the preheated oven.

Remove the chicken from the oven, rest for two minutes before serving.

To make the salad, roughly dice the tomato – nice big chunks and deseed and finely slice the red chilli.

Add the tomato and chilli to a large mixing bowl, along with the rocket, fresh basil, balsamic vinegar, olive oil and lime juice. Season well and toss ingredients together. Serve immediately.

To serve, pour cooking juices over the chicken and accompany with warmed ciabatta bread.

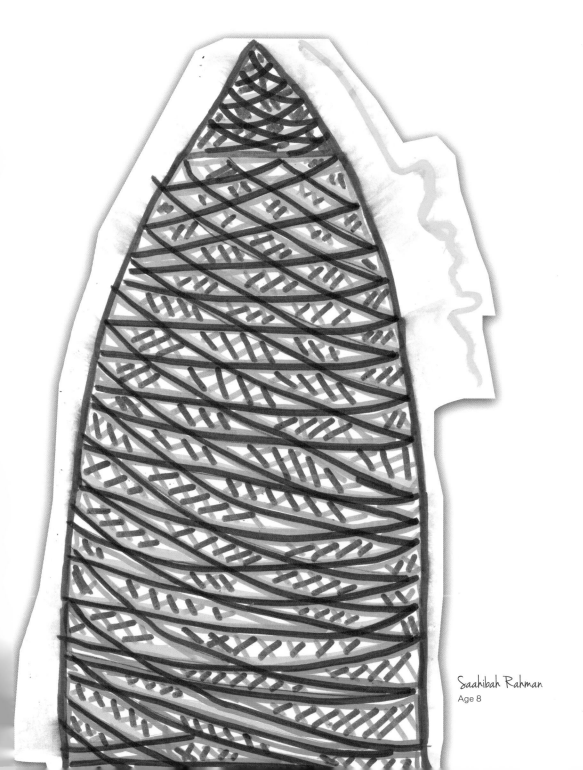

Saahibah Rahman
Age 8

Velimir Jakimovski
Age 10

Tandoori Chicken

"This has been made regularly in my family for the past 25 years or so! Back then, the only place we could buy tandoori powder was at the little oriental grocery stall in the market. Now you can get it easily in supermarkets. I've tried many variations over the years but the spice powder always give a much nicer result than tandoori paste from a jar."

Jane Davison, *Executive Assistant*

Ingredients
(Serves 4)
→ *1 chicken, quartered or equivalent chicken pieces (If using chicken breast, make sure it is on the bone otherwise it will be too dry. If you make extra, chicken thighs or legs reheat particularly well without drying for an easy after work dinner)*
→ *500 ml pot natural yogurt (can be low fat, Greek, whatever you prefer, all will work well)*
→ *2½ tablespoons tandoori spice powder*

Garnish
→ *1 red onion, peeled and thinly sliced*
→ *1 lemon, quartered*
→ *Fresh tomatoes*

Method
Begin by skinning the chicken if you like. I always do this as it makes the dish much less fatty. Make a couple of slits in each chicken piece.

Mix together the yogurt and tandoori paste in a bowl. Add more paste if you like hot chicken, less if you prefer mild.

Put the chicken in to a large plastic food bag then pour in the spicy yogurt. Make sure the chicken is properly coated and tie off. Marinate for a couple of hours in the fridge, ideally overnight (however this still works well if only left for a few hours).

Preheat the oven to 180°C or equivalent.

Remove the chicken and place in a baking dish. Pour any left over yogurt in the bag onto the chicken. Cover tightly with foil and cook in the top half of the oven for 1 hour or until properly cooked.

Remove the chicken from the dish. You'll be left with a watery liquid in the dish that can be thrown away. The chicken should be nicely coated with cooked yogurt.

Place the chicken onto a flat tray and brown under the grill until slightly charred and the yogurt coating has dried out a little. Cook the rice while you are doing this.

Serve with Basmati rice, sliced raw red onion and fresh tomato. Squeeze the lemon over the rice and chicken – it tastes particularly nice on the rice.

Nicky's Duck Supremo

"I developed this recipe after finding that restaurants never seemed to do duck quite how I liked it – so I just invented one to suit my taste. Also, the whole family love it, kids included"

Nicola Oliver, Research Consultant

Ingredients
(Serves 2)
→ *2 duck breasts with the skin on*
→ *1 chicken stock cube*
→ *2 good size glasses of white wine*
→ *2 tablespoons good quality cranberry sauce*
→ *Water as required*

Method
Place the wine and stock cube in a saucepan and bring to a gentle boil for about 10 minutes.

Add the cranberry sauce. Stir and top-up to a more fluid consistency with boiled water and simmer gently for another 10–15 minutes, whisking occasionally. You can also make a darker, fuller stock using red wine and substitute the cranberry sauce with dark, thick-cut marmalade. (You can prepare the sauce in advance and re-heat shortly before serving over the duck).

Score the skin side of the duck breasts. Season liberally with salt.

Preheat some oil in a heavy based frying pan. Add the breasts skin side down to seal for about 10 minutes, then turn over to the skin side for a further 10–15 minutes.

To help with timing and to cater to your own specific tastes, you can place in a preheated oven until you are ready to serve. Remove from the oven and rest for about five minutes before carving into slices.

Pour the well-heated sauce across the duck.

Serve with new potatoes, a herb salad and a dry rosé in summer and with dauphinoise potatoes and a bottle of Shiraz in winter.

Aurelia Brand
Age 9
Nicola and her daughter

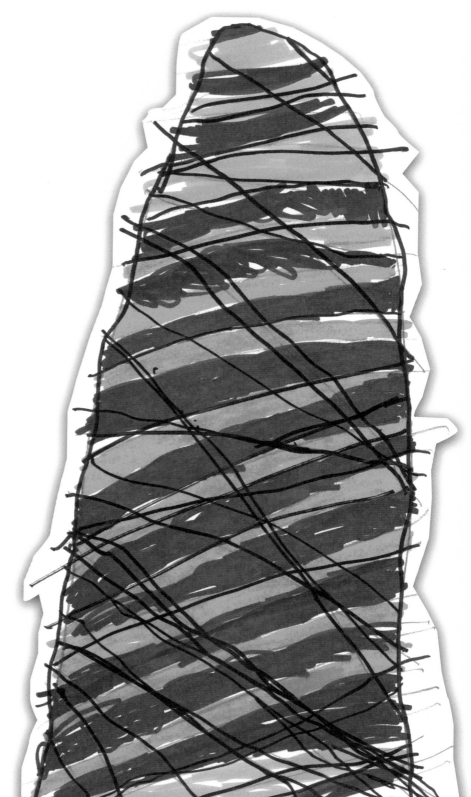

Karima Khatun
Age 6

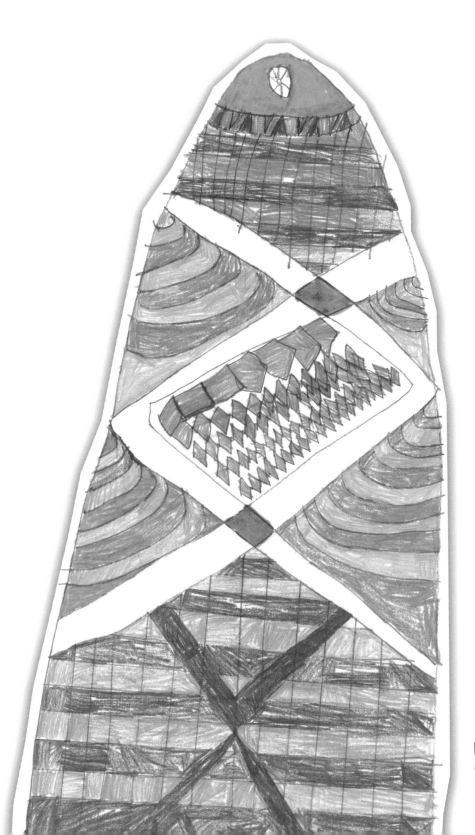

Iftekar Hussain
Age 8

Papet Vaudois (Vaudois Leek Hotpot)

"Here is a recipe which brings me back to my origins in the Canton of Vaud at Lake Geneva, it is actually exactly the recipe I got from my mother! I can expand on the beauty of Lake Geneva if you wish..."

Jean-Jacques Henchoz, CEO Reinsurance EMEA

Ingredients

(Serves 6)
→ *300 g Vaudois Saucisson (Vaudois sausage). Or a good quality smoked sausage*
→ *300 g Saucisse aux choux (sausage made of pork and cabbage) or a good quality pork and leek sausage*
→ *1 tablespoon butter*
→ *1 onion, chopped*
→ *1 garlic clove, chopped*
→ *1kg leeks, cut lengthwise, in approximately 4 centimetre wide sections*
→ *100 ml white wine*
→ *200 ml vegetable bouillon*
→ *500 g firm cooking potatoes cut into 3 centimetre cubes*
→ *½ teaspoon salt*
→ *Freshly ground pepper*

Method

Melt the butter over a low heat.

Fry the onions, garlic and leeks for approximately three minutes.

Add bouillon, white wine and potatoes, bring to a boil.

Reduce heat, season and add the vegetables.

Slice both the Saucisson and the Saucisse and place on the vegetables. Cover and cook on a low heat for approximately 45 minutes.

Towards the end of the cooking time, remove the lid and boil off some of the liquid.

To serve, arrange vegetables on a warm platter and top with the sausage sections.

Sausage Supper

"I was given the recipe by another mum who said it was a favourite with her family and so I thought I would give it a try. I have relied on it several times since then to provide supper for my own children and as a meal for hungry children on weekend camping adventures. It's so quick and tasty."

Christine Hill, *Manager Technical Accountant*

Ingredients
(Serves 4)
→ *450 g sausages (works with any sausages including meat free)*
→ *2 leeks*
→ *100 g mushrooms – cleaned and chopped*
→ *Small tin of sweetcorn*
→ *1 red pepper – cleaned and chopped*
→ *250 g pasta – preferably fusilli but any sort will do*
→ *284 g condensed mushroom soup*
→ *200 ml semi-skimmed milk*
→ *100 g Red Leicester cheese (grated)*
→ *25 g cheese and onion crisps*

Method
Preheat the oven to 150°C.

Slice the peppers and leeks and cook until tender.

Chop the mushrooms, add to the peppers and leeks and cook until tender. Add the sweetcorn.

Cook the pasta in boiling water for approximately seven minutes.

In a large saucepan mix together the soup and milk. Add the vegetables and bring the sauce to the boil, season to taste if required with salt and pepper.

Grill the sausages until lightly cooked, then slice.

Mix the pasta with the sliced sausages and put into an ovenproof casserole dish. Pour over the sauce.

Crush the crisps and sprinkle on top. Sprinkle with grated cheese.

Pop into oven until the cheese is melted – 150°C for approximately 15–20 minutes.

Serve with salad and garlic bread.

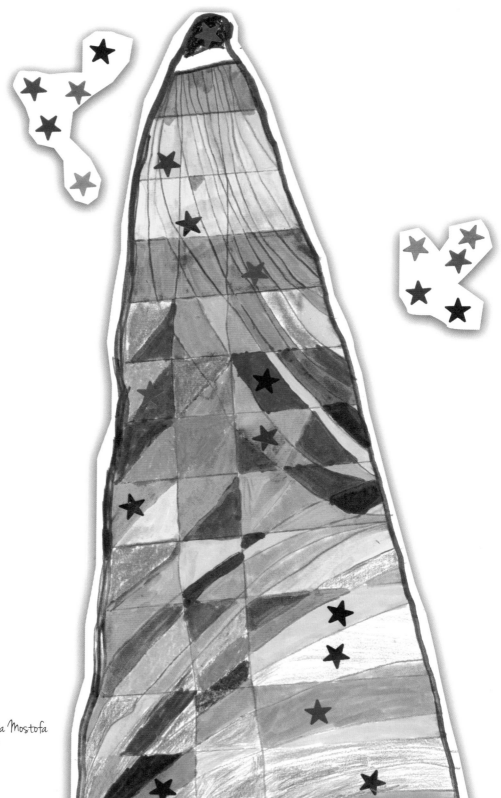

Nazia Mostofa
Age 8

Noah Hammam
Age 10

Flamekuche

"Here is my Luxembourgian contribution to the cookbook, one of my favourite recipes. Simple... and from the Alsace region of France where the other half of my family comes from."

Michel Liès, *Group CEO*

Ingredients
(Serves 4)
→ *250 g plain flour*
→ *200 g mushrooms*
→ *200 g cottage cheese*
→ *150 g smoked ham*
→ *3 eggs*
→ *50 g cheese, grated*
→ *25 g butter*
→ *1 cup crème fraîche*
→ *1 onion, chopped*
→ *½ teaspoon yeast*
→ *½ teaspoon salt*

Method
Preheat the oven to 170°C.

Stir in the yeast to the flour and add the butter, salt and half a cup of water then knead for ten minutes. Add water or flour as needed if the dough is too wet or dry. (Or you can buy ready-made shortcrust pastry.)

Roll out the dough and line a greased pie dish with it.

Stir fry the onions for three minutes, add the mushrooms and stir fry for a further four minutes.

Beat the eggs together with the crème fraîche, the cottage cheese and salt and pepper to taste.

Put a couple of tablespoons of the egg and cottage cheese mixture on top of the dough then cover with one third of the ham followed by half of the mushroom and onion mixture. Repeat this, then finish with a layer of ham.

Add the remaining egg and cottage cheese mixture as the final layer.

Sprinkle with cheese and bake for 40 minutes at 170°C.

Serve with fresh bread.

Natalia Hawson
Age 11
Drawing of Michel

Cape Malay Bobotie

"A quick simple meal which is delicious with a glass of white wine or an ice cold beer!"

Chanita Cross, *Executive Assistant*

Ingredients

(Serves 6)

Base
→ 1 kg minced beef (lean)
→ 2 slices bread (white)
→ 25 g butter
→ 2 onions
→ 2 garlic cloves
→ 6 bay leaves
→ 3 tablespoons sultanas
→ 2 tablespoons mango chutney (or peach)
→ 2 teaspoons madras curry paste
→ 1 teaspoon turmeric
→ 1 teaspoon salt

Topping
→ 2 large eggs
→ 300 ml milk

Method

Preheat the oven to 180°C.

Pour cold water over the bread and set aside to soak.

Chop the onions and fry in the butter for 10 minutes. Stir regularly until they are soft and starting to brown.

Crush the garlic and add both garlic and beef to the pan. Stir well – crushing the mince into fine pieces until it starts to change colour.

Stir in the curry powder/paste, herbs, spices, sultanas, chutney and two of the bay leaves. Add salt and plenty of pepper. Simmer in a covered pan for 10 minutes.

Squeeze the water from the bread then add to the meat mixture until well blended.

Tip into an oval dish (23 x 33 cm and about 5–6 cm deep.)

You can make the meat and bread base layer a day ahead and leave in fridge if that's helpful.

For the topping beat the milk and eggs, season to taste and then pour over the meat and bread mixture.

Top with the four remaining bay leaves and bake at 180°C until the topping is set and golden.

Serve with rice.

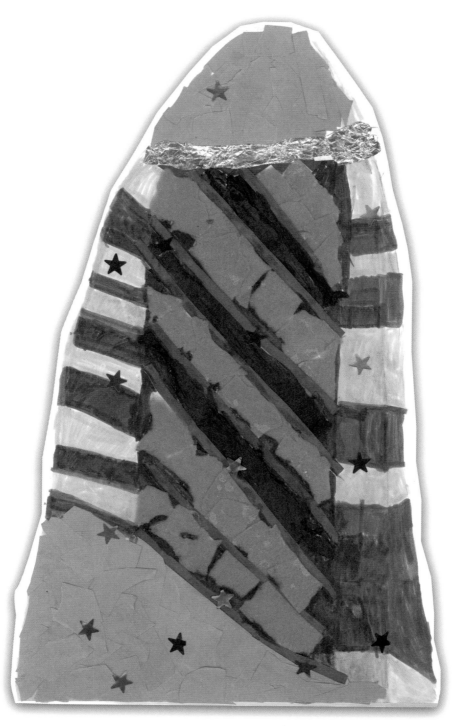

Nafiza Rahman
Age 9

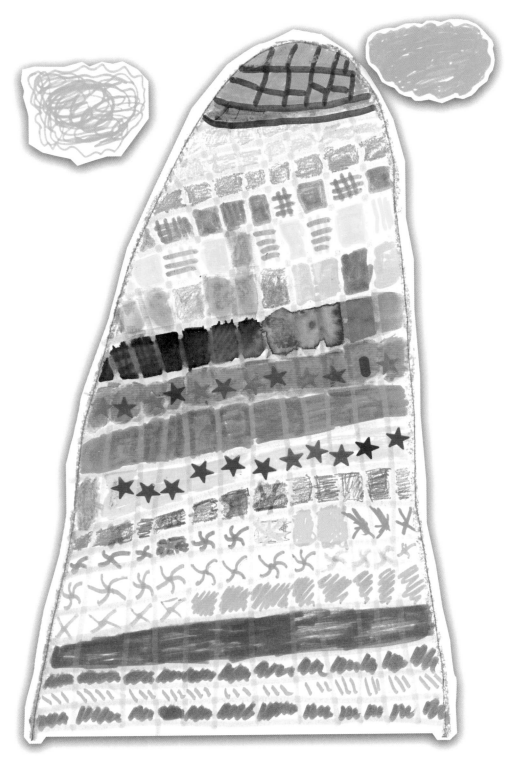

Muna Muse
Age 9

Hot Mexican Rice

"This recipe is a great time saver and delicious too. Quickly cooked in the microwave it can be adapted for vegetarians by using soya mince. You can make it as hot or not as you like, just adjust the chilli to taste."

Barbara Carmichael, *Head of Logistics Folkestone*

Ingredients
(Serves 4)
→ *1 lb minced beef (I use minced lean steak) or soya mince*
→ *15 oz can tomatoes*
→ *1 medium onion, chopped*
→ *1 medium green pepper, diced*
→ *1 small chilli pepper, chopped (I use 1 teaspoon chilli powder here)*
→ *1 clove of garlic, crushed*
→ *3.5 oz rice*
→ *4 oz seedless raisins*
→ *1 oz pine nuts*
→ *3 tablespoons oil*
→ *2 teaspoons salt*
→ *1¼ teaspoon pepper*

Method
Preheat a microwave browning dish (if you have one) on high for 4.5 minutes. (I don't have one and it works without).

Sauté the onion, green and chilli peppers, garlic and rice on high for 3 minutes. Stir every minute.

Mix in the beef and cook uncovered on high for 3 minutes, stirring frequently.

Stir in the remaining ingredients.

Cover and cook on high for 9–10 minutes until tender.

Leave to stand, covered for 10 minutes.

Fluff with a fork.

Serve with crusty bread.

Note: For ounces to grams conversion see chart on page 90

Marmite Meatballs

"This recipe converted my flatmate from someone who hates Marmite to someone who loves it. Great for a mid-week filling supper."

Will Wilson, *Financial Analyst*

Ingredients
(Serves 4)
→ *800 g lean mince beef*
→ *100 g breadcrumbs*
→ *3 x 400 g tins chopped tomatoes*
→ *1 x 400 g tin butter beans*
→ *2 large onions, finely chopped*
→ *2 garlic cloves, crushed*
→ *½ tablespoon cumin*
→ *½ tablespoon chilli powder*
→ *2 eggs, beaten*
→ *4 teaspoons Marmite*
→ *2 beef stock cubes, crushed*
→ *1 tablespoon rosemary (optional)*
→ *A couple of drops of Tabasco (optional)*
→ *Salt and pepper, to taste*

Method
Sweat one of the onions and one garlic clove in oil in a big pot until soft.

Meanwhile mix together the minced beef, the other onion and garlic clove, the eggs and the breadcrumbs along with the rosemary, cumin, chilli powder, salt, pepper and the two teaspoons of Marmite in a bowl.

Shape the mince mixture into 24 meatballs.

Add the meatballs to the pot and cook for 10 minutes until brown.

Add the chopped tomatoes, stock cubes, Tabasco, butter beans and remainder of the Marmite.

Turn the heat up and let it simmer until reduced (about 30–40 minutes), stirring periodically. Season to taste.

Serve with fresh tagliatelle and a hefty Shiraz.

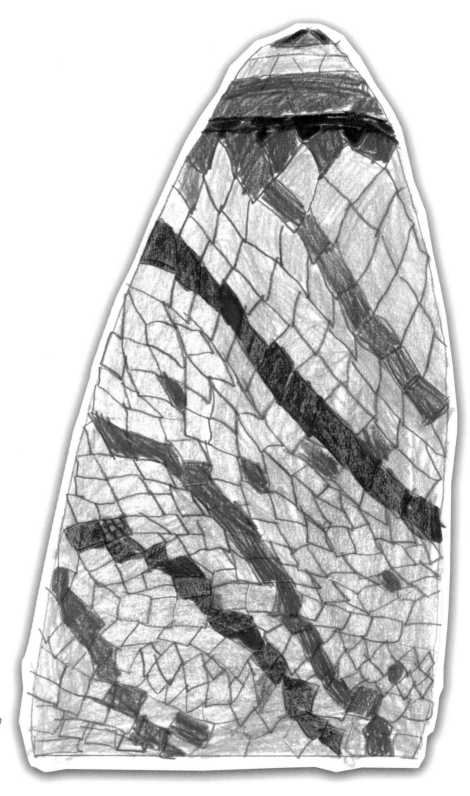

Samir Ahmed
Age 10

Kamal Shamat

Age 8

Moroccan Lamb

"This recipe is a great favourite with me and those I cook for. It is very flexible too and the ingredients can be adjusted to personal taste (substituting vegetables for meat, warming up the temperature with chilli flakes, add a clove of garlic, etc) without losing the lovely underlying flavours. It is a great supper dish for friends, as it will wait patiently, happily simmering, until you are ready to eat! Its origin is unknown – it has been passed around and tweaked along the way to arrive at this version, but no one seems to know quite where it started."

Anne McAllister, *Senior Business Analyst*

Ingredients
(Serves 4)
Part 1
→ *350 g lamb, bite-sized cubes*
→ *1 large onion, chopped*
→ *1 tablespoon olive oil*
→ *25 g butter*
→ *1 teaspoon ground ginger*
→ *1 teaspoon ground coriander*
→ *1 teaspoon cumin*
→ *1 teaspoon turmeric*
→ *½ teaspoon ground cinnamon*
→ *¼ teaspoon cayenne*
→ *Salt and pepper*

Part 2
→ *1 litre chicken stock*
→ *1 tin chickpeas, drained*
→ *1 x 400 g tin chopped tomatoes*
→ *1 red pepper, diced or strips*
→ *Juice of 1 lemon*
→ *Pinch of saffron*
→ *Tomato puree*
→ *Handful of sultanas*
→ *Handful of finely chopped dried apricots*
→ *2 large tablespoons spicy mango chutney*
→ *1 tablespoon chopped parsley*

Method
Fry the onion in oil and butter gently until translucent. Add the lamb and brown evenly.

Add the spices and salt and pepper from Part 1 and cook for a couple of minutes.

Transfer to a saucepan with ⅔ of the chicken stock, cover and simmer gently for one hour.

Add the rest of the ingredients from Part 2 and cook for a further 30 minutes. Add more chicken stock during this time if needed.

If you prefer a thicker sauce you can drain the chopped tomatoes and reserve the juice to add later if needed, or add a little couscous to thicken.

When ready to eat sprinkle with chopped parsley.

Serve with rice or couscous.

Cheese Puffs à la Joy!

"My Mother, Joy, has been making these for a million years and everyone loves them, they're delicious!"

Maryan Barnard, Assistant to Christopher McKechnie

Ingredients
(Makes 12)

Puffs
→ 1 cup grated mature cheddar cheese
→ 1 cup cake flour
→ 2 tablespoons baking powder
→ 1 large egg, beaten
→ A dash of cayenne pepper
→ Milk to blend

Filling
→ Two hard-boiled eggs mashed or grated
→ Half a cup of finely chopped onion
→ A dash each of cayenne pepper, paprika, garlic salt, black pepper
→ A little mayonnaise
→ Dash tomato juice
→ Some chopped parsley

Method
Preheat the oven to 180°C.

Mix all puff ingredients together with a little milk to make a soft dough.

Put portions of dough into patty pans* (small or large).

Bake in a hot oven for 10 minutes or so.

Makes about 12 large puffs – more if smaller patty tins are used.

For the filling, blend all ingredients together. Insert into the puffs.

Serve hot or cold.

*Patty pans are sold as jam tart baking trays in the UK
Note: For cups to grams conversion see chart on page 90

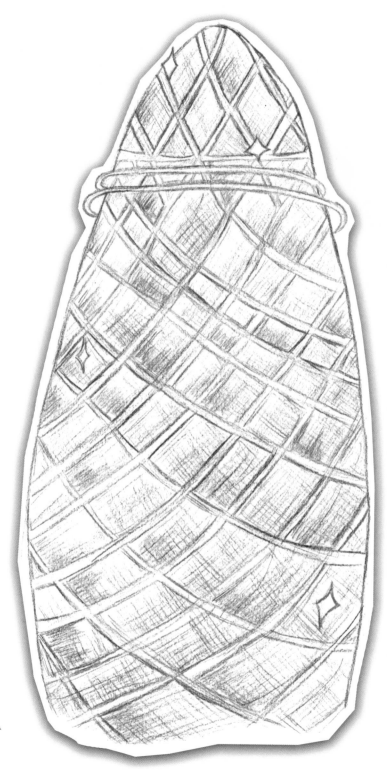

Nadia Hussain
Age 10

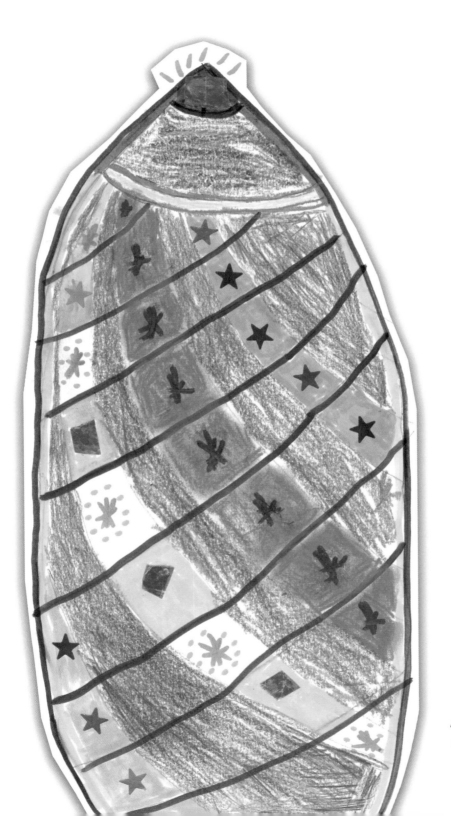

Maryam Mannan
Age 8½

Peanut Masala

"Peanut Masala is a popular Indian snack dish and is a fine accompaniment to main courses or as a snack for drinks, parties or just in front of the TV!"

Shane Thomas, *Senior Projects Manager*

Ingredients

→ *250g of skinless roasted salted/unsalted peanuts*
→ *1–2 medium or large red onions*
→ *Finely chopped coriander leaves*
→ *1–2 tablespoons lemon juice for taste*
→ *Salt (if the peanuts are unsalted)*
→ *2 green chillies (if you are feeling daring!)*
→ *Yogurt (adapted version only)*

Method

Chop the onions into small squares, no bigger than the peanuts.

Chop the coriander leaves into fine bits and put aside.

Take the skinless roasted peanuts – if these are whole you should split them apart. You can do this by putting them all into a mixing bowl and splitting them with your fingers or you can do it while they are in the package; just make sure you don't break them into very small pieces.

Put the split peanuts into a mixing bowl, add the chopped onions and the chopped coriander and using a spoon, mix well.

Now add a tablespoon of lemon juice to the mixture and mix it up again.

Garnish it with the coriander leaves and add the finely chopped chillies if you wish.

Your Peanut Masala is ready to be passed around to flatter taste buds!

An adaptation is to put in a blender with some yogurt for a more houmous style dip.

Fast and Delicious Lentil Soup

"This is a quick and tasty option for when I can't be bothered to spend a lot of time in the kitchen, and all the ingredients are usually already in the cupboard."

Tracy Cunningham, Senior Underwriting Consultant

Ingredients

(Serves 4)

→ *3 tablespoons butter*
→ *1 small onion*
→ *1 clove of garlic*
→ *1 cup green or red lentils (green hold their shape better)*
→ *400 g tin tomatoes*
→ *2 tablespoons tomato paste*
→ *3 cups chicken stock (or beef if you prefer a richer flavour)*
→ *Salt and pepper to taste*

Method

Finely chop the onion and crush the garlic.

Melt the butter in a saucepan over medium heat.

Sauté the onion first until soft. Add the garlic (do not burn or let it get crispy).

Stir in the lentils. Add the tomatoes, tomato paste and chicken stock and bring to the boil.

Reduce heat and simmer for 45 minutes or until lentils are soft and creamy.

Season with salt and cracked black pepper (and a squeeze of lemon if you like).

Serve with hot buttered toast.

Note: For cups to grams conversion see chart on page 90

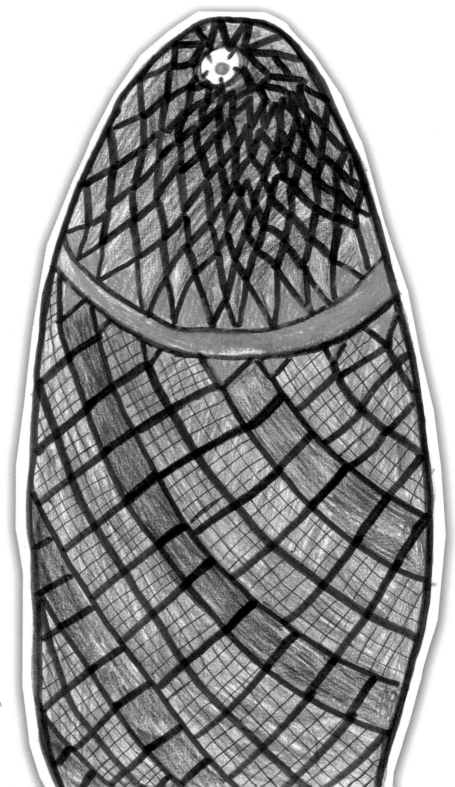

Tasnima Zaman
Age 10

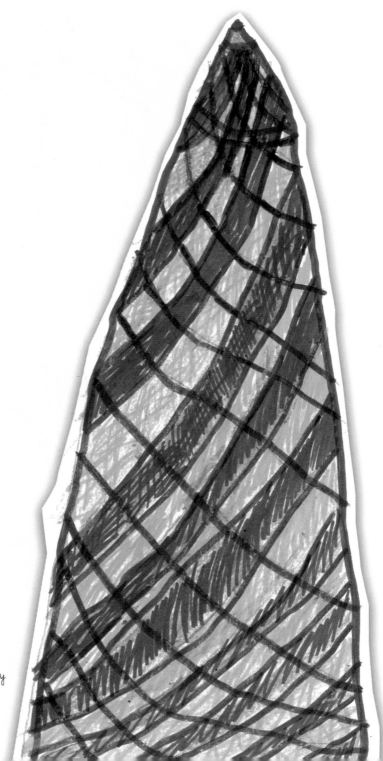

Xuan-Lan Mahtey
Age 6

Coconut Milk Pulao (Comfort in a Pot)

"One pot dishes always catch my eye because who has the time to slave over the stove? But if there are days when you crave for something really exotic and nice but don't want to struggle – here is the answer, Coconut milk Pulao! This recipe is heavenly. Quick to make and a great winner when you need a little 'pick me up' on a week night!"

Komal Ramamurthy, *Technical Accounting Administrator*

Ingredients
(Serves 4)
→ *2 cups basmati rice washed and soaked for 15–20mins*
→ *1 tin coconut milk*
→ *2 medium onions sliced*
→ *3–4 green chillies slit (optional – just a perforation to prevent it from bursting in oil yet providing a mild flavour)*
→ *4 whole cloves*
→ *2 cm piece of cinnamon (bark not the powder stuff)*
→ *1 teaspoon grated ginger and 1 teaspoon grated garlic*
→ *1 handful coriander leaves washed and chopped*
→ *1 handful of mint leaves washed and chopped (this can be left out if you don't like mint)*
→ *2 tablespoons oil/butter or a mixture of both if you want be good and bad at the same time!*

Method
In a saucepan, heat the oil/butter and add the cloves and cinnamon and when you see them sizzle add the green chillies and sauté for a few seconds. Then add the sliced onions and sauté some more, I like to add a big pinch of salt to get the onions going and the idea is to brown the onions a tiny bit as it makes them sweeter.

Once you see the onions go slightly brown on the edges add the ginger and garlic and sauté till the raw smell disappears. At this point add the coriander and mint leaves and sauté for a few seconds then add the soaked rice. Sauté for a few seconds gently without breaking the grains of the rice then add the liquid.

Normally when you cook rice the water ratio is 2:1. In this recipe, since we soaked the rice, we will use less liquid than we would have for regular white rice. Here I normally use about one and a half cups of coconut milk and two cups of water. This is flexible and you can use more coconut milk than water if you like. Bring the whole thing to a boil and taste the liquid to adjust the seasoning.

The water should taste a bit salty as the volume will increase as the rice cooks. Once you are happy with the seasoning, cook the rice as you would normally – either in a saucepan or in a rice cooker.

Serve hot with poppodoms, pickle and raita. And Enjoy!

Note: See cups to grams conversion table on page 90

Ananya Ramamurthy
Age 7
Drawing of Komal

South African Rusks

"Feel free to be creative with this recipe – you can add a mixture of sunflower seeds, pine nuts and pumpkin seeds, chopped nuts or even raisins. Another tip is that I use three separate loaf tins and then freeze the third loaf for another time."

Anabela Pinto, Executive Assistant to Head of Financial Risk Management

Ingredients
→ 300 g butter
→ 2 cups brown sugar
→ 1 cup oil
→ 2 large eggs
→ 2 cups buttermilk
→ 1 cup wholewheat flour
→ 3 cups bran (from the cereal aisle in the shops- just crush the cereal)
→ 1 cup nuts or seeds (and in this case use 1 cup less of bran)
→ 1 kg self-raising flour
→ 1 teaspoon salt

Method
Preheat the oven to 180°C.

Mix the butter and sugar until creamy.

Add all other ingredients, keeping some of the seeds back, and mix thoroughly.

Put mixture into lightly greased loaf tins and sprinkle remaining seeds on the top.

Bake at 180°C for 60 minutes.

Allow to cool then slice into two cm wide soldiers and cook again on a very low heat oven, around two hours at 50°C.

They will become nice and crunchy.

Serve with a variety of toppings or on their own.

Note: For cups to grams conversion see chart on page 90

Fariha Nowsheen
Age 11

Tahmid Habib
Age 8

Nashera Begum
Age 6

Desserts

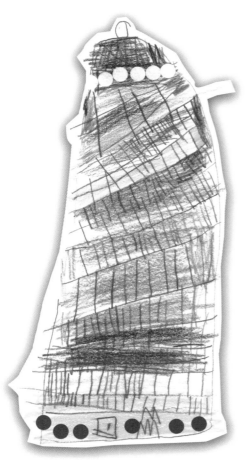

Aaron Armstrong-Silva
Age 8

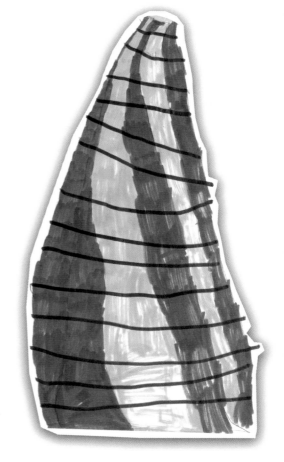

Fabiha Rahman
Age 6

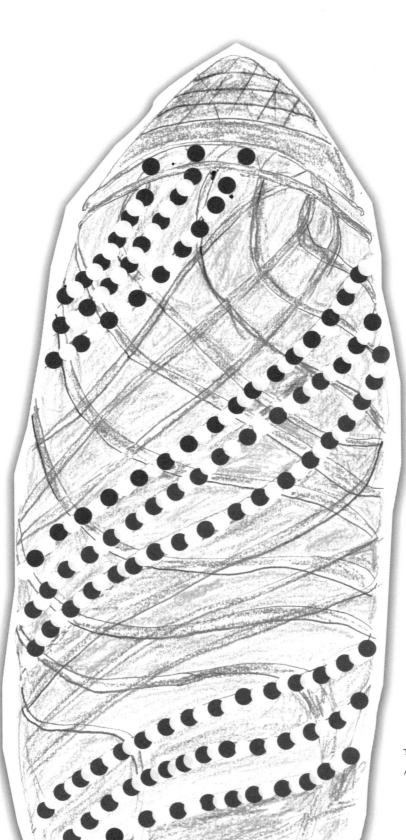

Rima Begum
Age 11

Mrs Oxford's Aussie Banana Bread

"Having lived in Australia for 4 years, I thought I'd introduce a great Australian tradition into this cookbook – Banana Bread. This comes from a friend's Mother (Thanks Maureen!) and represents the best Banana Bread recipe that I have come across. Banana Bread is best enjoyed the day after baking, as it tends to firm up and become more solid then, so is easier to slice. Try it toasted with butter."

Russell Higginbotham, *CEO Swiss Re UK & Ireland*

Ingredients
→ *1 cup plain flour*
→ *1 cup self-raising flour*
→ *1 cup brown sugar*
→ *½ cup of milk*
→ *2 eggs beaten*
→ *120 g butter*
→ *4 bananas*
→ *1 tablespoon white vinegar*
→ *1 teaspoon baking powder*
→ *1 teaspoon bicarbonate of soda*
→ *1 teaspoon vanilla essence*

Method
Preheat the oven to 180°C.

Mix all ingredients together in a large bowl.

In a separate bowl, roughly mash three to four bananas.

Mix the contents of both bowls together.

Pour into greased large loaf tin and bake at 180°C for approx 45 minutes to 1 hour (depending on your oven).

Check it is cooked by sticking in a skewer and making sure it is clean when you take it out.

Serve sliced and toasted with butter.

Note: For cups to grams conversion see chart on page 90

Amelie Higginbotham
Age 6
Drawing of Russell

Apple and Toffee Crumble

"We tend to find that we end up with a lot of apples in September/October and this is a great way to eat them and vary the flavours. Keep the mix and apples the same and change what you include with them, whether it's toffee, pear, apricots or blueberries."

Steve Yelland, *Accountant*

Ingredients
(Serves 4–6 people)
→ *1 lb cooking apples*
→ *8 oz plain flour*
→ *4 oz butter*
→ *6 oz brown sugar*
→ *Pinch of nutmeg*
(optional)
→ *400 g condensed milk*

Method
Preheat oven to 170°C.

Mix the flour, butter and 5 oz of the sugar in a large mixing bowl until all ingredients are crumbly. As an optional step you can grate and stir in a small amount of nutmeg to taste at this point.

Peel, core and slice the apples and place in the base of a casserole dish and add the remaining 1 oz of sugar.

Pour the condensed milk on top of the apples, this will turn into toffee. (Other options at this point are to add other fruit such as pears, blackberries, dried apricots or sultanas instead of the condensed milk.)

Sprinkle the crumble mix on top of the condensed milk or fruit.

Level the top and place in the oven at 170°C for 30–40 minutes.

Serve hot – on its own or with custard or cream.

Note: For ounces to grams conversion see chart on page 90

Mekhi Douglas-Chang
Age 4

Yaseen Haque
Age 5

Linzertorte

"This is what you need most to get a hearty Linzertorte: blackberry jam and love. The rest of the ingredients can vary."

Stefan Gloeckler, Head Media Production, Zurich

Ingredients
→ 200 g flour
→ 125 g fine raw sugar
→ 125 g unsalted butter
→ 125 g ground almonds
→ 2 eggs
→ 1 sachet of vanilla sugar
→ 1 teaspoon cinnamon powder
→ 2 pinches of ground clove
→ 2 drops of almond flavouring
→ 1 pinch of salt
→ 1 level teaspoon baking powder
→ ½ tablespoon Kirsch (cherry schnaps)
→ Some lemon zest
→ 380 g blackberry jam

Method
Preheat oven to 180°C.

Mix the flour and baking powder into a circle on a flat surface.

Add all the other ingredients (except for the blackberry jam and one of the eggs) and work your way while kneading from the middle to the outer end of the circle until you get a dough.

Chill the dough for at least half an hour.

You need ¾ of the dough for the Linzertorte base. Roll out the dough and line a greased round baking tin (26 cm diameter) with it and prick with a fork.

Now spread the jam across the dough.

Shape the remaining dough into strips and lay them on top of the jam in a basket weave design. Paint with the remaining beaten egg.

Bake in the oven at 180°C for 40–50 minutes.

Coconut and Jam Tarts

"This recipe is originally from my Mum in South Africa, which I tweaked a little to suit ingredients in the UK. It has been a family favourite for years in my home – one frequently requested by my friends."

Anneline Vermeulen, Claims Examiner

Ingredients
(Makes 12)

Base
→ 2 cups flour
→ 2 teaspoons baking powder
→ Pinch of salt
→ 125 g butter
→ 4 egg yolks
→ ¾ cup hot water
→ ¼ cup sugar

Topping
→ 2 cups desiccated coconut
→ 4 egg whites
→ 1 cup of sugar

Filling
Approximately ½ jar strawberry (or any red berry) jam

Method
Preheat oven to 180°C.
Grease muffin tin trays with butter.

Put flour, baking powder, salt, sugar and butter into a big mixing bowl and mix with your fingers.

Separate eggs into a bowl of whites and a bowl of yolks. Add boiling water to the egg yolks and beat with a fork for a minute.

Add the egg yolk water mixture to the bowl with dry ingredients and using a spatula mix thoroughly.

Then place even amounts of this mixture into the 12 muffin tin bases and using fingers, ensure mixture is even at sides and bottom.

Place a heaped teaspoon of strawberry jam into middle of each base.

Add egg whites, sugar and desiccated coconut into a bowl and mix.

Scoop a heaped tablespoon of mixture onto the top of the bases already filled with strawberry jam.

Place muffin trays into preheated oven for 30 minutes at 180°C.

Allow to cool before removing from muffin trays.

Enjoy!

Note: For cups to grams conversion see chart on page 90

Heeba Tahisn
Age 8

Maariyah Ahmed
Age 5

Fruit Cake

"The earliest cake I remember eating was my mother's fruit cake. They were immensely popular with my family and frequently didn't last until they were cold. Often I would have a slice warm from the oven with milk poured over to cool it to an eating temperature. Regardless of the amount of fruit my mother had put in, our constant reprise to her was to add more fruit. Finally, after several iterations of the recipe she had to complain that if she added any more in, the cake would no longer hold together!"

Chris Jack, *IT Developer*

Ingredients
→ *2 lb of your favourite dried fruit. Typically this is 1 lb of currants, ⅓ lb each of sultanas and raisins and a couple oz each of cherries and mixed peel. These can be substituted for whatever you have available, be it dried prunes, cranberries, pineapple, apricots, dates or even grated carrot*
→ *8 oz salted butter*
→ *8 oz brown sugar*
→ *8 oz plain flour*
→ *4 eggs*
→ *Optional spoonful of treacle*
→ *Up to 2 teaspoons mixed spice*
→ *Up to 2 teaspoons nutmeg*
→ *Up to 2 teaspoons ginger*
→ *Up to 2 teaspoons ground cardamom*
→ *Up to 2 teaspoons cinnamon*
→ *Brandy*

Method
Soak the dried fruit in brandy overnight.

In the morning mix the butter and sugar and add the spices.

Preheat oven to 140°C.

Beat the eggs and add along with the flour, if you fancy, fold in a spoonful of treacle.

Mix in the fruit and place in a greased 8 inch cake tin. Cover and tie round with brown paper with a small hole in the middle to let out steam. Then cook at 140°C for around four and a half hours.

Check whether the cake is cooked by seeing if a knife inserted in the middle comes out clean.

When cool (if it hasn't been eaten already) keep it in a cupboard: feeding it with brandy from time to time.

Personally I have my fruit cakes without covering, but when it's time to eat you can cover your cake with marzipan, royal icing or apricot jam.

Mini Upside Down Blueberry Cakes

"These make a wonderful dessert or a perfect accompaniment to coffee. They can be made really quickly and are best served hot. (My family and friends protest they like them cold too, I don't know how they know this though as they always seem to disappear shortly after leaving the oven!) I always keep some blueberries or raspberries in the freezer so I can make them if we have visitors arriving unexpectedly."

Tee Dobinson, *The Gherkin Guru*

Ingredients
(Makes 18)
→ *6 oz self-raising flour*
→ *6 oz butter*
→ *6 oz dark brown sugar*
→ *3 large eggs*
→ *1 teaspoon baking powder*
→ *½ teaspoon vanilla essence*
→ *400 g fruit (this is approximate – you can really put masses in and I use whatever we have around)*

Method
Preheat the oven to 180°C.

Sieve the flour into a mixing bowl and add the brown sugar.

Melt the butter completely and add to the bowl.

Beat the eggs and add the vanilla essence, add to the bowl. Mix everything together.

Add the fruit (you can use blueberries straight from the freezer if you need to).

Spoon into mini muffins cases (the silicon ones are brilliant).

Cook for about 15 minutes at 180°C (Keep the oven door closed for as long as possible – just check towards the end of the time.)

Take them out of the oven and leave them in their cases for five minutes.

Turn upside down into individual dishes.

Serve while still warm. Crème fraîche optional.

Note: For ounces to grams conversion see chart on page 90

Lamiya Khanum
Age 8

Ben Morris
Age 12
Drawing of Tee
'The Gherkin Guru'

Sarah's Carrot Cake

"Here's my Gran's recipe for her delicious Carrot Cake."

Kirsty Howden, *Claims Specialist*

Ingredients
Cake
→ *8 oz wholemeal self-raising flour*
→ *8 oz grated carrots*
→ *4 oz butter*
→ *4 tablespoons honey*
→ *4 oz Demerara sugar*
→ *2 oz walnuts*
→ *1 tablespoon lemon juice*
→ *2 teaspoons cinnamon*

Topping
→ *4 oz icing sugar*
→ *2 oz cream cheese*
→ *1 oz butter*
→ *½ teaspoon vanilla essence*

Method
Preheat the oven to 180˚C.

Melt together the butter, honey and sugar.

Mix together all the dry ingredients. Add the carrots, the melted mixture and the lemon juice.

Put into a lined 1½–2 lb loaf tin and bake at 180˚C for one hour.

Place on a wire tray to cool.

Mix all the topping ingredients together and spread on the top of the cake once it has completely cooled.

Note: For ounces to grams conversion see chart on page 90

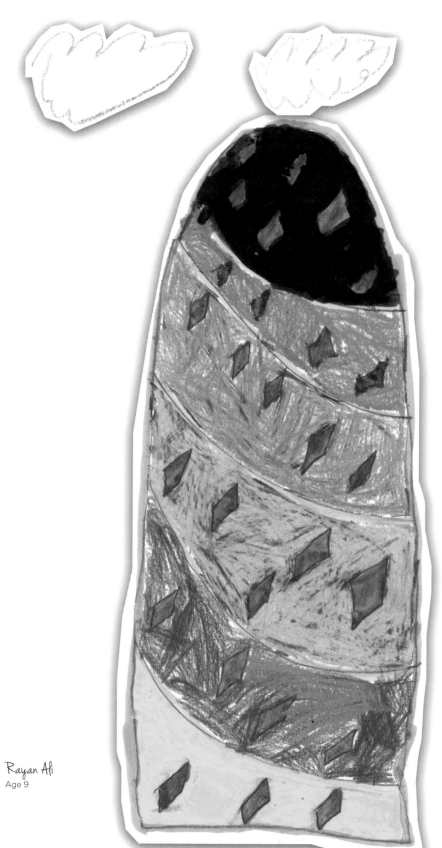

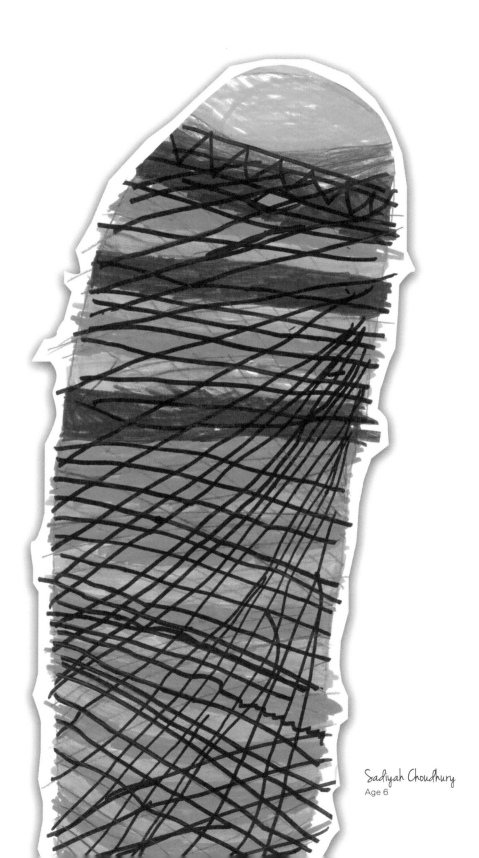

Sadiyah Choudhury
Age 6

Nan's Rotten Cake

"This is my Nan's recipe for cheesecake. As children we always called it 'Rotten Cake' because whenever anyone asked what it was my Grandad would say 'You don't want that, it's rotten' to try and deter us from eating it so there was more for him!"

Hannah Manning, *Business Manager*

Ingredients
Base
→ *8 oz digestive biscuits*
→ *4 oz butter*

Topping
→ *1½ lb curd cheese*
→ *8 oz caster sugar*
→ *2 eggs*
→ *1 teaspoon vanilla essence or sultanas or lemon juice*

Method
Preheat the oven to 150°C.

Crush the biscuits, melt the butter and mix together.

Press into a 9" buttered cake tin and leave to chill in the fridge.

Cream the sugar and curd cheese together.

Add the eggs one at a time, add the flavouring of your choice. Beat well.

Pour mixture onto the biscuit base.

Cook in oven for 50 minutes at 150°C.

Leave to cool. Place in fridge for a further two hours before serving (or ideally make one day in advance).

Serve on individual plates (and watch out for Grandad!)

Note: For ounces to grams conversion see chart on page 90

Marina Pearce
Age 9
Drawing of Nan and Grandad

Mars Bar Cheesecake

"Here's my Mum's Mars Bar Cheesecake recipe. Now … just to eat it!"

Charlotte Sharp, Executive Assistant

Ingredients
Base
→ 140 g unsalted butter
→ 200 g digestive biscuits, crushed

Topping
→ 4 large Mars bars
→ 250 g Philadelphia cheese (or Mascarpone)

Method
Grease a 22.5 cm loose bottom flan tin.

Make the base by melting the unsalted butter (you can do this in the microwave). Stir in the crushed biscuits and mix well. Place in the flan tin, pressing down to ensure the base is evenly spread. Refrigerate while you make the topping.

Roughly chop up three of the Mars bars and either melt in a bowl over (but not touching) a saucepan of boiling water or melt in the microwave. Keep an eye on it. If you melt the Mars bars too fast they will separate out and then go solid!

When melted, take off the heat and add the Philadelphia cheese or Mascarpone, stirring well until incorporated.

Chop the remaining Mars bar into small pieces and add to the mixture.

Put into the flan tin on top of the digestive biscuits, smooth down and chill until required.

If you want it to look fancy dust with cocoa powder before serving.

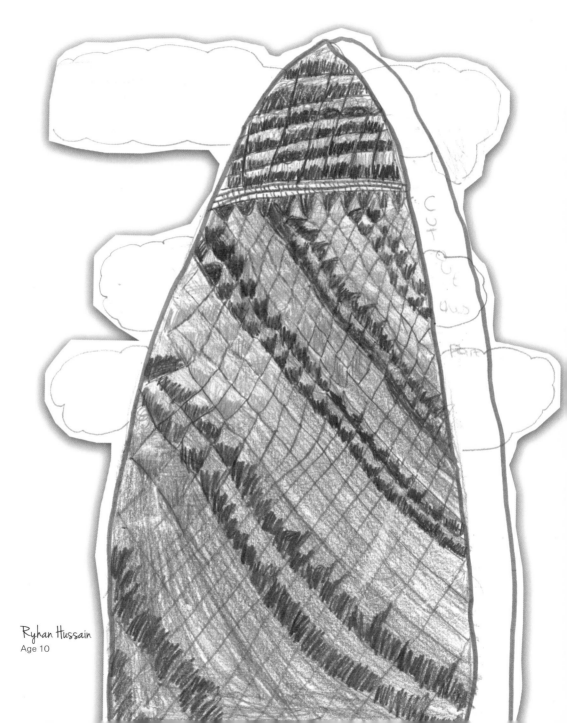

Ryhan Hussain
Age 10

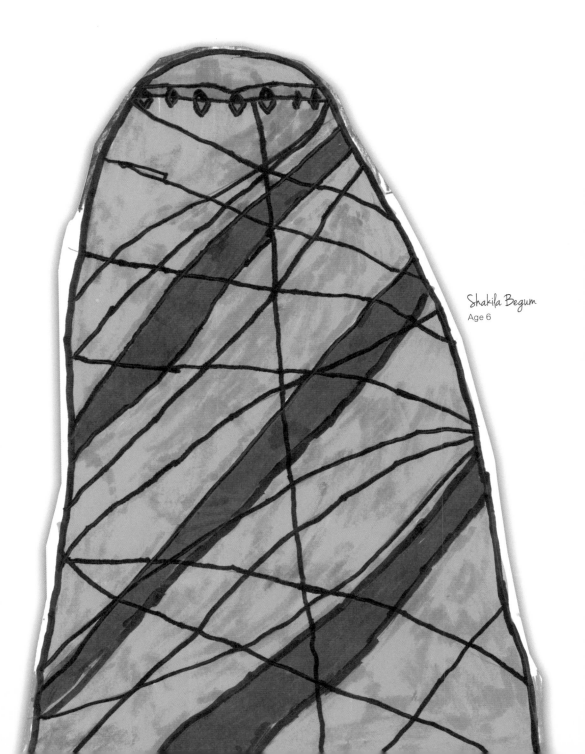

Shakila Begum
Age 6

Double Chocolate Cheesecake

"This is simple but delicious! With the new craze for Chocolate Philadelphia it is a great chance for people to experiment with a new ingredient!"

John Carte, *Team Leader Folkestone*

Ingredients

Base
→ *300 g bourbon biscuits*
→ *60 g unsalted butter*
→ *50 g plain chocolate*

Filling
→ *2 tubs Chocolate Philadelphia*
→ *250 ml double cream*
→ *60 g icing sugar*
→ *1 teaspoon vanilla extract*
→ *handful of milk chocolate chips*

Decoration
→ *handful of white and milk chocolate chips*

Method

Place all ingredients for the base into a food processor & blitz until they begin to clump together.

Pour the mixture into a loose-bottomed flan tin, pressing the mix up the tin edges. Refrigerate for at least an hour, or place into freezer for 30 minutes.

Mix the Chocolate Philadelphia with the vanilla extract and icing sugar until smooth and completely combined. Add the chocolate chips.

Whisk the cream until it forms soft peaks, taking care not to over beat.

Fold the cream into the Chocolate Philadelphia mix, pour into the biscuit base. Work the filling into the edges of the base, then smooth the top with a palette knife.

Cover loosely with foil then chill for three hours or overnight.

To serve, remove the cheesecake from the tin and scatter with the milk and white chocolate chips.

The Most Dangerous Cake in the World

"This recipe is for a chocolate mug cake. Why is it the most dangerous cake in the world? Because now you are only five minutes away from a delicious chocolate cake at any time of the day or night..."

Rebecca Younan, Claims Specialist

Ingredients
(Serves one but can be shared between two)
→ 4 tablespoons flour
→ 4 tablespoons sugar
→ 2 tablespoons cocoa
→ 3 tablespoons vegetable oil (preferably not olive) or butter
→ 1 large egg or 2 small eggs
→ 3 tablespoons milk
→ 3 tablespoons white chocolate chips (or chocolate buttons, almonds or fudge)
→ A small splash of vanilla extract
→ 1 large coffee mug (microwave safe)
→ A microwave!

Method
Add the flour, sugar and cocoa to the mug and mix well.

Add the egg(s) and mix again thoroughly.

Pour in the milk and add the oil or butter and mix again.

Add the chocolate chips and vanilla extract and mix one more time.

Put your mug in the microwave and cook for 3–5 minutes. (Adjust time to suit your microwave.)

The cake will rise over the top of the mug, but don't be alarmed!

Allow to cool a little and tip onto a plate.

Serve on its own with cream, ice cream or custard – eat!

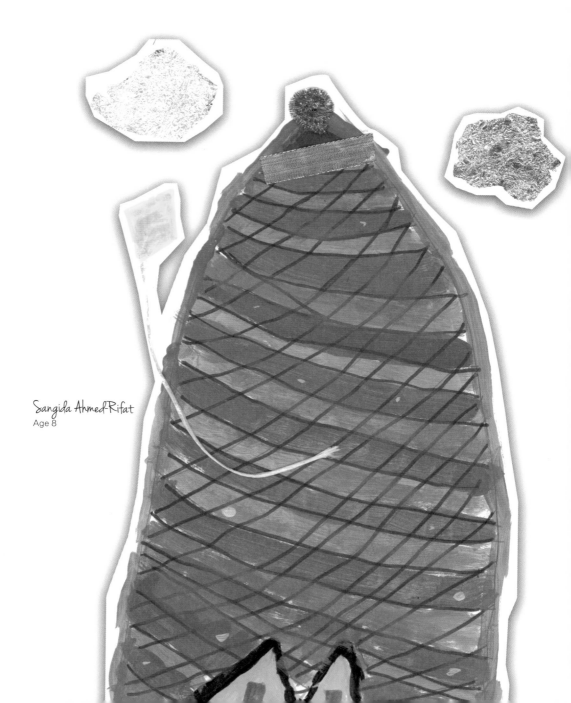

Sangida Ahmed-Rifat
Age 8

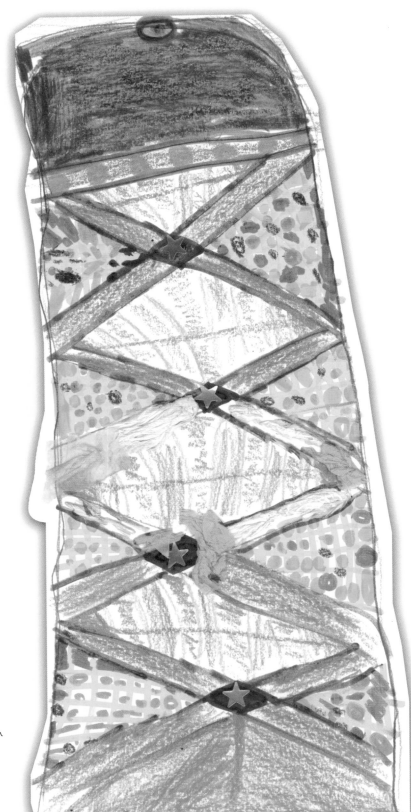

Aaliyah Begh
Age 8

Delicious Chocolate Crunch

"This simple recipe is a real family favourite, the ingredient amounts are very forgiving if you want to throw it all together quickly and it tastes like it takes much more effort than it does!"

Evelyn White *(sent in by Sean White, Senior Underwriter)*

Ingredients

→ *1 packet of Rich Tea biscuits*
→ *6 oz butter*
→ *6 oz best quality dark chocolate you can get*
→ *4 oz best milk chocolate you can get (substitute for all dark chocolate if you prefer)*
→ *6 oz golden syrup*
→ *2 oz cocoa*
→ *3 oz raisins*
→ *1 teaspoon salt*

Method

Melt the butter with 4 oz of the plain chocolate and all the golden syrup. Mix in the cocoa.

Place biscuits in a large sealed bag and bash with a rolling pin until crushed.

Add biscuits, raisins and salt to the chocolate mix. Stir well.

The mix should be fairly wet – if it looks a bit dry add more butter and golden syrup to moisten.

Place the mix in a 8" square tin, push down until flat and completely filling all parts of the tin.

Melt remaining chocolate in a bowl and pour over the chocolate and biscuit mix. Cool until set, then tip out of tin and cut in squares. Yum!

To keep fresh, store in a sealed container in the fridge.

Marshmallows, nougat or honeycomb can be added to the basic chocolate mix. Be inventive!

Note: For ounces to grams conversion see chart on page 90

World's Best Cookies

"These cookies are so quick and easy to make and taste lovely! Usually made for when friends and family come round to visit or for the team at work as a Monday morning treat! Plus these are always good for the odd bake sale at school and work!"

Rachael Humphreys, *Client Manager GA & Aerospace UK*

Ingredients
→ *150 g self-raising flour*
→ *100 g softened butter*
→ *100 g soft brown sugar*
→ *50 g chocolate chips*
(you can increase this up to 80 g if you like!)
→ *1 tablespoon golden syrup or honey*
→ *½ teaspoon vanilla extract*

Method
Preheat the oven to 170˚C.

Beat the butter, sugar and syrup together until soft and creamy.

Mix the flour, vanilla extract and add the chocolate chips.

Divide the mixture into walnut-size lumps and place onto greased baking tray, but don't flatten them.

Bake for between 8–13 minutes depending on your oven.

Leave to cool on the tray for a couple of minutes, then remove and place on to a wire rack to finish cooling.

Variations are: 'White Chocolate and Cranberry Cookies' – use 50 g of white chocolate chips and 50 g dried cranberries and 'Double Choc Chip Cookies' – replace two tablespoons of flour with two tablespoons of cocoa.

James Humphreys
Age 6
Drawing of Rachael

Shannur Rahman
Age 10

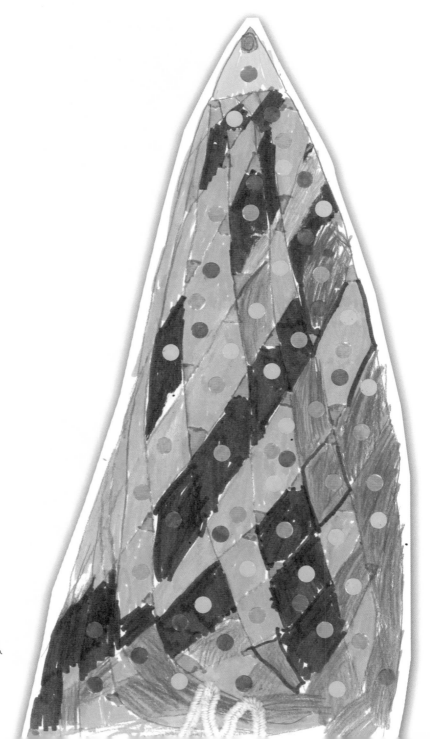

Bleona Zejnullah
Age 5

Amaretti Biscuits

"This is incredibly simple and makes loads."

Jennifer Gandy, Company Secretary and Executive Assistant, Legal Reinsurance EMEA

Ingredients
→ 4 egg whites
→ 340 g caster sugar
→ 340 g ground almonds
→ 2 or 3 drops almond extract
→ Rice paper

Method
Preheat the oven to 180°C.

Whisk the egg whites into mounds.

Stir in the caster sugar and ground almonds.

Mix and add a few drops of almond extract.

Form the mix into small biscuit shapes or balls.

Place on rice paper (on top of baking trays).

Cook for about 10 minutes at 180°C.

Leave to cool.

Serve with coffee.

Energy Boosting Flapjacks

"We all really love these flapjacks, they are really easy for the kids to make with a little help, and delicious to eat. They are a great snack for re-fuelling our active/sports mad boys and go really well with a cup of tea for me! Daddy likes them after a long run too!"

Richelle Sullivan (sent in by Simon Sullivan, Claims Manager)

Ingredients
(Makes 12)
→ 150 g Swiss muesli
→ 150 g porridge oats
→ 225 g butter
→ 75 g brown sugar
→ 4 tablespoons honey
→ 150 g mixed dried fruit or sultanas or chopped dried apricots or cranberries...

Method
Preheat the oven to 180°C.

Grease a baking tin (28 x 18 cm) with a little butter.

Put the butter, brown sugar and honey in a pan over a low heat. Stir together until the butter has melted and the sugar has dissolved.

Take the pan off the heat and stir in the Swiss muesli, porridge oats and all the dried fruit, mixing well.

Spread the mixture into the tin and press it down with the back of a spoon.

Bake the flapjacks for 20–25 minutes, take care not to overcook them or they will taste too dry.

Cut the mixture into 12 pieces and leave them in the tin to cool completely before removing.

Ayrton Sullivan
Age 6
Drawing of Richelle

Davis Csimbala
Age 10

Conversion Chart

Ideally use all metric or imperial measures, as they are not necessarily interchangeable.

½ oz	15 g
2 oz	60 g
4 oz	120 g
6 oz	180 g
1 lb	450 g
1 pint	570 ml
1 cup flour	150 g
1 cup sugar	175 g
1 cup uncooked rice	200 g
1 cup grated cheese	110 g
1 cup butter	225 g
1 cup sultanas/nuts	150 g
1 cup liquid	240 ml

Celsius	Farenheit	Gas Mark
140	275	1
150	300	2
170	325	3
180	350	4
200	400	6

Please adapt temperatures and timings for fan ovens as necessary.

Acknowledgements

Russell Higginbotham had the brilliant idea of raising funds for the NSPCC via a Swiss Re staff cookbook after seeing his friends and colleagues in Swiss Re Australia do something similar. It was on a cold London morning over a cup of coffee that Russell and Lorraine Sage decided they didn't feel that a traditional Swiss Re design would work for this book and hatched the idea of using children's illustrations. Russell has kept a keen interest in the project throughout and Lorraine has kept her eye on everything with her usual combination of efficiency and charm. Both have been a joy to work with.

The project couldn't have succeeded without their Swiss Re colleagues. Donatella Fiala in the Legal Team has given invaluable advice, Orla Harte was our exacting proofreader and Stefan Gloeckler, Andreas Preis and the team at Media Production are responsible for the beautiful design of the book. We particularly appreciated Stefan's constant enthusiasm and the fact that he took the arrival of 218 Gherkins on his desk in Zurich without missing a beat!

We greatly appreciate the support of Sarah McQueen and Searcys | The Gherkin, of headteacher Catherine Morgans-Slader and her staff at William Davis Primary School and of all the recipe testers.

Special thanks to gourmet Sara Fox for her expert advice.

Finally a huge thank you to everyone who contributed recipes and illustrations – we couldn't have done it without you!

The Editor
Swiss Re asked Tee Dobinson to realise the project for them and she has done a fantastic job of compiling and editing the book and co-ordinating all the Gherkins.

Motivational speaker Tee is the author of three books, including '360° at the Gherkin' and is co-founder of the bespoke publishing company Baizdon. Tee was christened the 'Gherkin Guru' for her expert knowledge of the building and its views and, as Searcy's official speaker on The Gherkin, gives talks at lunches and events at the top.
www.teedobinson.com

Cover:
Yana Mahmood *Age 6*

First inside page: drawings beginning from top left:
Manazar Dahir *Age 9,* **Quhhar Abdul** *Age 10,* **Maryam Begum** *Age 3,* **Yusuf Ahmed** *Age 6,* **Musa Khaleed** *Age 4,*
Naseem Husain *Age 10,* **Mohima Begum** *Age 10,* **Zahra Haque** *Age 7,* **Zabib Abdul** *Age 11,* **Azizah Hussain** *Age 8,*
Wadidha Sharjana *Age 5,* **Sofian El Hassani** *Age 6,* **Shamimah Begum** *Age 9,* **Aliyah Hussain** *Age 5,*
Ibrahim Mohammed *Age 6,* **Mustafa Ali** *Age 7*

Right hand side page: drawings beginning from top left
Hafsa Begum *Age 6,* **Shaan Khan** *Age 11,* **Mahirul Amin** *Age 8,* **Yunus Monowar** *Age 6,* **Alexsandar Jakimovski** *Age 6,*
Yahya Ahmed *Age 11,* **Eshita Uddin** *Age 9,* **Mazhar Hussain** *Age 10,* **Arif Ali** *Age 8,* **Neshad Ahmed** *Age 7,*
Fowzia Sultana *Age 6,* **Zaedul Ohi** *Age 8,* **Kereshma Ghulamghous** *Age 7,* **Abu-Tahir Muhammed** *Age 3,*
Amelie Higginbotham *Age 6*

Published by Swiss Re Services Ltd

Edited by
Tee Dobinson

Designed by
Swiss Re, Logistics/Media Production, Zurich

Printed by
Central Printers

This book is printed on sustainably produced
paper. The wood used comes from forests
certified to 100% by the Forest Stewardship
Council (FSC).

06/12, 2000 en